# BBC Earth
# DO YOU KNOW?
## Level 3

# UNDERWATER FORESTS

Inspired by BBC Earth TV series and developed with input from BBC Earth natural history specialists

# Written by Blake Hoena
# Text adapted by Catrin Morris
# Series Editor: Nick Coates

LADYBIRD BOOKS

UK | USA | Canada | Ireland | Australia
India | New Zealand | South Africa

Ladybird Books is part of the Penguin Random House group of companies
whose addresses can be found at global.penguinrandomhouse.com.
www.penguin.co.uk    www.puffin.co.uk    www.ladybird.co.uk

Penguin
Random House
UK

First published 2020
001

# Contents

# New words

algae

forest

grass

land
(noun)

leaf
(leaves)

oxygen

rock

root

seaweed

shallow

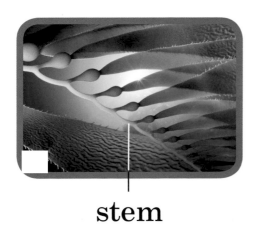

stem

underwater

# What grows under the water?

Plants grow in many places. There are flowers in a garden and trees in a **forest**.

Some plants grow under the water. We call them **underwater** plants. There are more plants in the sea than on the **land**.

Kelp is a kind of **algae**. Some underwater kelp forests are very tall.

There are many phytoplankton in the sea. Phytoplankton are very, very small plants.

Seagrass grows on the sea floor.

**THINK!**

Do you know any plants that grow under the water?

# Why are underwater forests important?

Underwater forests are important for animals and people. The plants and algae can be food or homes for animals.

Many small animals eat underwater plants and algae. These small animals are food for bigger animals.

Green sea turtles eat seagrass.

People need underwater plants and algae, too. Some people eat kelp.

People make shoes and furniture from seagrass. Seagrass is also put on fields to help people grow food.

**LOOK!**

**Look at the pages.**
Why is seagrass useful?

Plants use the sun to make food.

They make **oxygen**, too, which all animals need to live.

Small phytoplankton in the sea make a lot of oxygen.

This octopus is looking for crabs to eat in a kelp forest.

This cuttlefish is looking for other cuttlefish in the **seaweed**.

Small fish are safe from bigger fish in the **roots** of mangrove trees.

▶ **WATCH!**

**Watch the video (see page 32).**
How does the kelp forest help the octopus to hide?
How does the octopus catch the crab?

# What eats phytoplankton?

There are lots of phytoplankton in the sea. Many animals eat phytoplankton.

Phytoplankton can make the sea green.

Krill are very small animals that eat phytoplankton. Bigger animals eat the krill.

Humpback whales eat krill. Whales have big mouths. They can eat a lot of krill!

## PROJECT

**Work in a group.**
Use books or the internet to find three kinds of whales that only eat very small animals and krill. How many small animals do they eat every day? Draw each whale and write its name underneath.

# What are kelp forests?

Kelp is a kind of algae. You can find it in cold water near land.

Many plants begin to grow when it is sunny. Kelp does, too.

Kelp can grow into thick and very tall underwater forests.

air bladder

Kelp has air bladders that help it grow up to the top of the water.

Sea otters sometimes sleep in the kelp. It helps them to stay in one place.

▶ WATCH!

**Watch the video (see page 32).**
Why does kelp grow up to the top of the water?
Why do lots of animals live in the kelp?

15

# Why are sea urchins bad for kelp forests?

Some animals are bad for underwater forests.

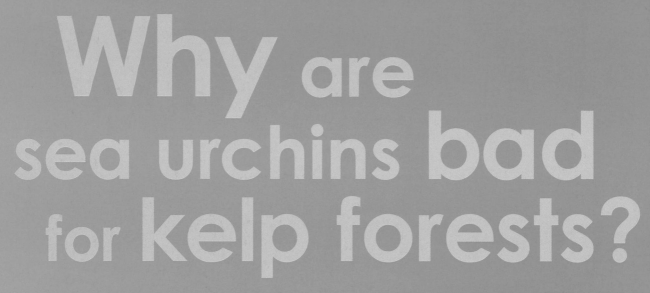

Sea urchins eat a lot of kelp. Then, there is nothing for other animals to eat or live in.

sea urchin

Some animals help underwater forests.

Garibaldi fish move sea urchins. They do not want the sea urchins to eat all the kelp where they live.

Sea otters help the kelp forests, too. They eat the sea urchins.

📖 **FIND OUT!**

**Use books or the internet** to find out how many teeth sea urchins have.

# What is seagrass?

Most plants have roots, **leaves** and a **stem**. Seagrass does, too.

In some places, there is a lot of seagrass.

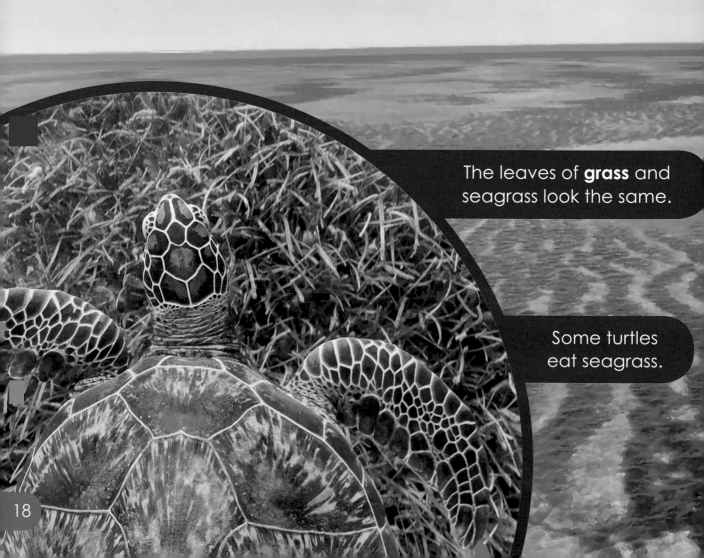

The leaves of **grass** and seagrass look the same.

Some turtles eat seagrass.

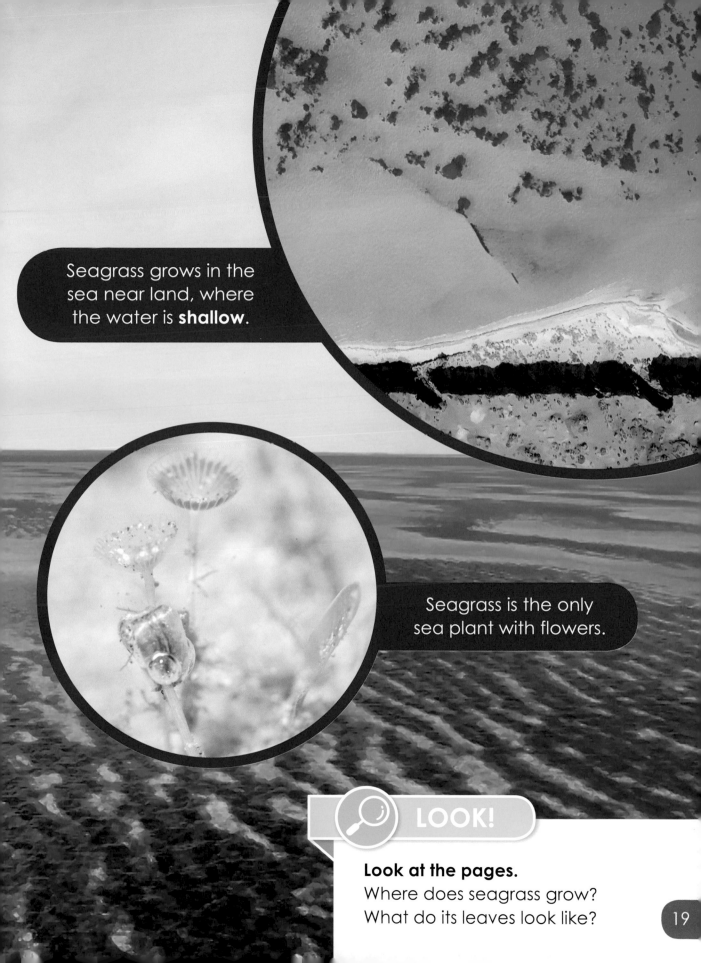

Seagrass grows in the sea near land, where the water is **shallow**.

Seagrass is the only sea plant with flowers.

**LOOK!**

**Look at the pages.**
Where does seagrass grow?
What do its leaves look like?

# Why are sharks good for seagrass?

Many animals live in seagrass. Sometimes there is not a lot of seagrass for other animals because green sea turtles eat it.

Tiger sharks also live near the seagrass and they eat green sea turtles.

Green sea turtles can eat a lot of seagrass every day.

The turtles have to swim or the sharks can eat them.

When the turtles are swimming from the sharks, they can't eat much seagrass.

**THINK!**

When the sea turtles move, does this help them, too? How?

# HOW are kelp and seagrass different?

Kelp and seagrass live on the sea floor, but they are different.

Seagrass has roots that grow into the sea floor.

Most seagrass is green.

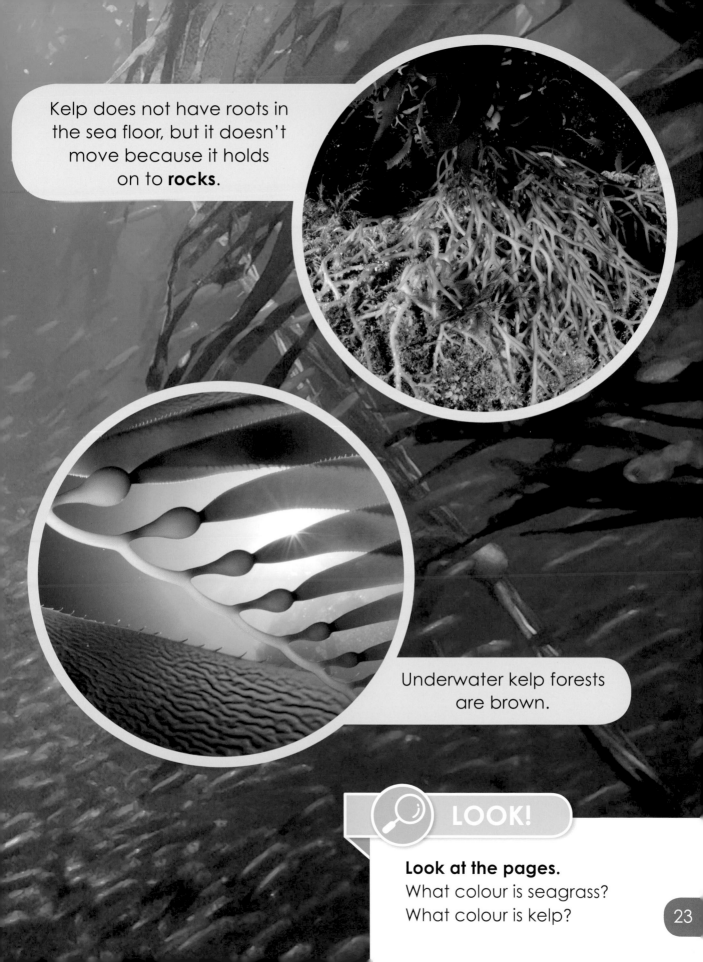

Kelp does not have roots in the sea floor, but it doesn't move because it holds on to **rocks**.

Underwater kelp forests are brown.

**LOOK!**

**Look at the pages.**
What colour is seagrass?
What colour is kelp?

# What are mangrove forests?

Mangroves are trees. You can find them in seawater near land.

Part of the tree grows above the water, but the roots grow under the water.

Small fish can swim safely in mangrove roots.

There are bigger animals near. They look for food, but they cannot swim in the roots.

There are shrimps in the sand near the mangrove roots, too.

When the fish swim past, the shrimps can catch them.

▶ WATCH!

**Watch the video (see page 32).**
Where do mantis shrimps live?
How long do they live with their mates?

# How do seadragons live in underwater forests?

Weedy seadragons are very small animals that live in underwater forests. They are safe there. They look like seaweed.

Other animals cannot see the weedy seadragons. They only see seaweed.

This father seadragon carries the mother seadragon's eggs.

**Seadragon babies come out of the eggs in the underwater plants.**

The young seadragons live near shrimps, their favourite food!

**THINK!**

**Use books or the internet** to find out about dragons.
Why do you think the animal on this page is called a seadragon?

# What other animals live in underwater forests?

Underwater forests are full of big and small animals.

They all want to be safe and find food.

shrimp

There are very small mysid shrimps in the seaweed.

A shark is waiting near the roots of a mangrove tree.

Fur seals are swimming across the kelp forest.

Lots of spider crabs are visiting the seagrass.

**LOOK!**

**Look at the pages.**
What different animals can you see in the underwater forests?
How many different kinds of animals are there?

# Quiz

**Choose the correct answers.**

**1** Kelp is a kind of . . .
  **a** animal.
  **b** algae.
  **c** flower.

**2** Phytoplankton are . . .
  **a** very small plants.
  **b** very small animals.
  **c** very small fish.

**3** What do people NOT use seagrass for?
  **a** for making furniture
  **b** for helping to grow food
  **c** for eating

**4** Kelp lives in . . .
  **a** hot water.
  **b** warm water.
  **c** cold water.

**5** Sea urchins eat . . .
  **a** kelp.
  **b** Garibaldi fish.
  **c** sea otters.

**6** Which sentence is NOT true?
  **a** Seagrass grows in the sea.
  **b** Seagrass grows on the land.
  **c** Seagrass grows near the land.

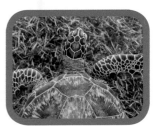

**7** Tiger sharks eat . . .
  **a** seagrass.
  **b** green sea turtles.
  **c** kelp.

**8** Which does NOT have roots?
  **a** a mangrove tree
  **b** seagrass
  **c** kelp

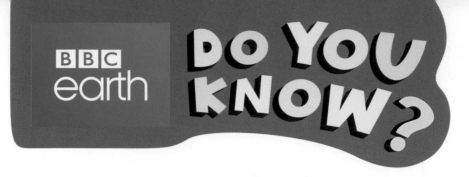

**BBC earth**

**DO YOU KNOW?**

Visit www.ladybirdeducation.co.uk for FREE **DO YOU KNOW?** teaching resources.

- video clips with simplified voiceover and subtitles
- video and comprehension activities
- class projects and lesson plans
- audio recording of every book
- digital version of every book
- full answer keys

**To access video clips, audio tracks and digital books:**

1 Go to **www.ladybirdeducation.co.uk**
2 Click "Unlock book"
3 Enter the code below

HHga5UCwbL

**Stay safe online! Some of the DO YOU KNOW? activities ask children to do extra research online. Remember:**

- ensure an adult is supervising;
- use established search engines such as Google or Kiddle;
- children should never share personal details, such as name, home or school address, telephone number or photos.